WISE UP: GRANNIES ADVICES

Delay equals disobedience

First eBook Edition: June 2019

Copyright © P. Marimi & S. Masundire

Artist: Paul Maposa

Design: E. Masundire

To the teacher/parent

Wise up: Grannies advices are short stories designed to equip school pupils with reading skills and to introduce them to the use of proverbs. The environment in which we grow in today does not promote the perpetual use of proverbs. These booklets therefore seek to hook the minds of children as they read them and instill the use of proverbs. They also provide a unique approach to the teaching of both reading and spelling for pupils.

Helping the child to learn reading is a gradual, repetitive and cumulative process which if not well handled may be a blow to the child's ego. The tireless reading needed to transform the child may be so cumbersome to the extent of driving him away from books. The **Wise up: Grannies advices** series however are designed to draw the children's attention to books. There are 14 booklets in this series providing a variety good enough to kill any sense of straying monotony. They provide well illustrated and interesting content. Besides being a source of entertainment, they also create and stimulate creativity in pupils thereby laying out a good foundation for creative writing and storytelling in children.

The children can use the books under the guidance of both the teacher at school and the parent at home. Involvement of the teacher and parent to the child's learning creates a supportive and encouraging atmosphere which is a necessity to every child. It is important for the teacher and parent to know that each book can be read many times by the learner. This strengthens the pupil's vocabulary as they go through each book.

Delay equals disobedience

This is Auntie Rose and Mercy. Sam is Mercy's brother. They both stay with Auntie Rose.

Auntie Rose has baked a cake. The cake is delicious. It is fluffy and sweet. Auntie Rose is good at baking sweet fluffy cakes. She uses many sweet ingredients.

The cake is set on top of the table. Auntie Rose has also prepared some tea. She wants to use some milk for the tea. Hot milky tea tastes delicious with a cake.

There is Sam and Mercy. They enjoy outdoor games. Sam is playing with his ball. Mercy is working with her play dough.

Auntie Rose is calling out for the children to come into the house. She has prepared a cake and some tea.

Mercy quickly responds to Auntie's call. Sam is busy playing with his ball. He ignores Auntie's call. He is enjoying his ball game.

Mercy is happy and enjoying the cake and some
tea. Sam is still playing his ball game outside.
He is not aware of the delicious cake.

At last Sam decides to come into the house. He is late. Mercy has already eaten his share of the cake.

Delay equals disobedience.

Read

1. Brother
2. Stay
3. baked
4. delicious
5. fluffy
6. prepared
7. taste
8. outdoor
9. working
10. children
11. enjoying
12. busy
13. aware
14. decide
15. already

16.equals
17.disobedience
18.delay
19. ingredients
20. dough
21.quickly
22. respond
23. ignore
24. serve
25. share

Activities:

Complete these sentences

dough   delicious   Sam   aunt

outdoor   brother

1. Rose is an ---- to Mercy.

2. Sam is a ---- to Mercy.

3. Aunt baked a ---- cake.

4. The children enjoy ---- games.

5. Mercy was working with her play ----.

6. ---- enjoys ball game.

Match the opposites

brother	bad
sweet	early
many	go
outdoor	sour
come	sister
good	few
on top	indoor
late	under

Word building

1. fl-
2. -ou-
3. -ous
4. sh-
5. dis-

Make your own sentences

1. both
2. bake
3. table
4. taste
5. game

Answer these questions

1. Who stays with Auntie Rose?

2.What does Auntie Rose use to bake cakes?

3. How do you describe Auntie Rose's cakes?

4. Where did Auntie set the cake and the tea?

5. Who ignored Auntie's call?

6. Draw yourself and your friends playing the game you love most.

Discuss

1. What do you call these people: your mother's father, your father's sister, your mother's sister and a child from your mother's sister?
2. What are the ingredients for a cake?
3. Where do we get milk from?
4. Why do children sometimes disobey?
5. How should you help a disobedient friend to be obedient?
6. What do you think parents should do to make children obey?
7. What type of games can you play alone?
8. What are the benefits of games to children?
9. Is it a good habit to eat someone's share of food?
10. What sort of things can we share with others at home and at school?

Story Telling

1. Imagine your own story and tells the day you missed a meal whilst playing a game.
2. Describe in detail the process of baking a cake.

3. Look at the picture and describe how you would decorate it to fit your birthday cake wish.

Decision making

1. How should you react to an instruction?
2. What should you do to balance your work and play time?
3. How do you help others to obey?
4. Why is it bad to ignore parents and guardians?
5. What dangers can befall children who disobey?

Meal planning

1. What is your favorite meal of the day?
2. What do you like about meal preparation?
3. How do you prepare your favorite meal?
4. Which one of your day's meal would you not mind to miss or share?
5. How do you serve a meal at home?

Life Application

1. Think of a way you can suggest to encourage other children to be obedient and share with your friends.
2. Write a story about the dangers of disobedience.

Training Techniques to the parent/guardian/teacher

Defiance or disrespect are common problems amongst children of all age groups. However, no stage in child development is too late to effect change and discipline. We need wisdom, love and care to help the children. Following are help tips:

a) Investigate the possible causes of defiance and disrespect
b) Confront the child and engage
c) Withdraw privileges.
d) Communicate with the child the way to work through area of discord.
e) If needed engage professional help.
f) Continue to show love, concern and care